72 Hour Bag
Making Your Own Personal Survival Kit

Stephen B. Fraser

Copyright © 2012 Fraser Enterprises

ISBN: 1484010086
ISBN-13: 978-1484010082

DEDICATION

This book is dedicated to my father who taught me the most important thing is to always be prepared.

CONTENTS

CHAPTER 1

WHAT IS A 72-HOUR BAG?

A 72-Hour Bag is a portable kit that contains the items one would require to survive for at least seventy-two hours when evacuating from a disaster. The focus of a 72-hour bag is on evacuation and short term survival. Other names for such bags are "Grab Bag", a "Go Bag", a "Battle Bag", a "PERK or Personal Emergency Relocation Kit", a "GOOD or Get Out Of Dodge Bag", and "BOB or Bug Out Bag".

While it might sound similar to a survival kit; Survival kits are typically a package of basic tools and supplies prepared in advance as an aid to survival of an emergency. Survival kits come in a variety of sizes, contain supplies and tools to help a person with basic shelter against the elements, help them keep warm, meet their health and first aid needs, provide food and water, signal to rescuers, and assist them in finding their way back to help. Supplies in a survival kit normally contain a knife, matches, tinder, first aid kit, fish hooks, sewing kit, and a flashlight.

The primary purpose of a 72-Hour bag is to allow one to evacuate quickly if a disaster should strike. It is therefore prudent to gather all of the materials and supplies that might be required into a single place, such as a bag or a few storage containers. The recommendation is that a 72-Hour bag should contain enough supplies for at least seventy-two hours. This arises from advice from organizations responsible for disaster relief and management. The typical response time can take up to seventy-two hours to reach people affected by a disaster and offer help. The bag's contents may vary according to the region of the user. Someone evacuating from the path of a hurricane may have different supplies than someone one that lives in an area prone to tornadoes or wildfires.

In addition to allowing one to survive a disaster evacuation, a 72-Hour bag may also be utilized when sheltering in place as a response to emergencies such as blackouts, tornadoes, and other severe natural disasters. A 72-Hour bag is essential for almost any emergency. Your 72-Hour bag could mean the difference between life and death.

There are many types of disasters and emergencies: floods, fires, earthquakes, hurricanes and tornadoes. In many cases, a 72-Hour bag will be sufficient. It is estimated that after a major disaster, it may take up to three days for relief workers to reach an area. It could take even longer to reach all areas affected. In the case of a disaster where you might be waiting for help for longer than 72 hours, it would be wise to consider a kit that you could live on for 7-10 days. If you live in a disaster prone area a 72-Hour kit is the minimum you should have available. You should plan your 72-Hour kit according to your family size.

There are plenty of places you can find and purchase a 72-Hour bag or kit. While these kits are adequate, they are also generalized and designed to be a one size fits all. I am not suggesting that there is anything wrong with these kits. The problem with this solution is that buying a kit will only contain the basics one would need. A true 72-Hour bag or kit needs to be personalized for each person. That being said there is no reason not to buy a kit as a base and add to it.

No matter what there are a few things that you need to consider when creating a 72-Hour bag.

1) Your 72-Hour bag should be portable.

2) It should be stored in an easily accessible area close to your escape route.

3) Each Family Member should have their own 72-Hour bag with food, clothing and water.

4) Enclose damageable items in air and waterproof bags to protect them.

5) Personalize your 72-Hour bag so that it fills the needs of each family member.

6) Inspect your 72-Hour bag at least every six months. Make sure that you check your medications. Check children's clothing for proper fit. Adjust clothing for winter or summer needs. Check your batteries, light sticks, food and water.

7) Consider the needs of the elderly or other people with special needs when building your 72-Hour bag.

CHAPTER 2

WHY DO YOU NEED A 72-HOUR BAG?

Think about where you live. Think about the types of natural disasters that could happen in your area. Depending on your location you may be more likely to have certain natural disasters than other areas. For example where I live in North Idaho I am less likely to have a Hurricane as opposed to someone living in Florida. Events such as wildfires, flooding, and microbursts can happen pretty much anywhere. There are also blizzards and ice storms in areas that have a true winter season.

What do all these events have in common? Simply put when they happen they usually happen without advance warning. Often they all cause large scale damage and interruption to infrastructure and services. Even in those times when there is a warning they are usually in the form of grab and go. Rarely do you have the luxury of six or eight hours to get things together.

When these events do happen sometimes the damage and destruction is minor, while other times it is catastrophic. They can take out utilities like power, water, and gas delivery. They interrupt sanitation and medical services. It often takes days or weeks just to restore basic services. Preparing for the worst case scenario that never occurs is always better than reacting after it happens.

All public entities prepare for the worst case scenarios. Police, Fire, and EMS services hold mock drills so that in the event that the worst case scenario does happen they can manage it. Many people don't prepare and as a result when the event does come they often don't fare as well as others.

Consider for a moment if we had a major incident that resulted in a major disruption to electrical services. Incidentally most people would say well I would just ride it out. Granted most power disruptions only last a few hours. Let's say it lasts two days and we don't know if it will be back on in another day or not. Think about everything in your house that runs on electricity. We have no lights, no refrigeration, no TV, no radio, no hot water, and no heat. Granted you might say I have a gas stove and gas furnace. Most furnaces don't work when electricity is disrupted because the thermostat operates on electricity as do the igniters on gas stoves. Now its day three the food in the refrigerator and freezer is spoiling, you haven't showered in two days and the toilet don't work anyway because the pumps that supply water pressure stopped working when the power went out. So you finally decide to leave. You jump in your car and realize you only have a half tank of fuel. You drive off and go to the gas station but you can't get gas because the pumps run on electricity too. You start driving not knowing which way to head only to find that the roads are littered with vehicles that have run out of gas.

You may be thinking that is a lot of what if's, but it is a scenario that is very capable of happening. There are very few things that you come into contact with daily that don't use electricity. And if you imagine taking away one little component it causes a ripple effect. Now granted you may never be in a situation like this, but if and when it does arrive you will be happy you are prepared to handle it.

The popularity of shows like Revolution and to a lesser effect The Walking Dead, Tend to make people think about what if this really happened, how would I react, and what would I do? The over whelming thing is that more often than not most people are either not prepared or under prepared. Sadly the unprepared usually resort to looting and other means to survive.

CHAPTER 3

THE BEST 72-HOUR BAG TYPE

To answer the question about what is the best 72-Hour bag depends a lot on your situation. If you are like me, and you want the most functional, then you can optimize your choice and make one size work for any situation. If you're not that fortunate, you may need to optimize for different places like one for your home and another for your car. You will also want to take into consideration your physical strength. Your ability to carry one for any distance when fully loaded can be a real concern. Especially when the situation turns into one where your only mode of transportation is your own two feet.

There are many factors and choices when selecting your best 72-Hour bag. First consider what and how much you are going to need to carry. Second consider how you are going to carry it. I have seen people who have made their 72-Hour bag in a large plastic tote. There is no right or wrong choice here. It will all depend on your perceived situation and needs. Personally I tend to prefer to use a backpack for my 72-Hour bag. The reason behind this is there is no guarantee that I will be able to use my car to get to safety. In all actuality in every possible scenario I come up with it all ends in me having to don my gear and walk out to safety.

There are many options when looking for a backpack for a 72-Hour bag. Backpacks in general fall into one of three categories: frameless, external frame, and internal frame. A pack frame, when present, serves to support the pack and distribute the weight of its contents across the body more appropriately, by transferring much of the weight to the hips and legs. Most of the weight is therefore taken off the shoulders, reducing the chance of injury from shoulder strap pressure, as well as being less restrictive of the upper body range of motion.

Frameless – Is the simplest backpack design, it is comprised of a bag attached to a set of shoulder straps. Such packs are used for general transportation of goods, and have variable capacity. The simplest designs consist of one main pocket. This may be combined with webbing or cordage straps, while more sophisticated models add extra pockets, waist straps, chest straps, padded shoulder straps, and padded backs. These packs are generally produced inexpensively.

External Frame – These External frame packs were designed to carry heavier loads. They do this by giving the wearer more support and protection and better weight distribution than a frameless strapped bag.

The frame of an external frame pack is typically made from aluminum, other lightweight metal alloys, or reinforced synthetic polymers or plastic. It is equipped with a system of straps and tautly-stretched netting which prevents contact between the metal frame and user's back. In addition to comfort, this "stand-off" provides the additional benefit of creating air circulation between the frame and the wearer's back. External frame packs are generally cooler than internal frame designs. External frame packs have a fabric "sack" portion which is usually smaller than that of internal frame packs, but have exposed frame portions above and below the sack to accommodate attachment of larger items. In addition, the sack can often be removed entirely, permitting the user to customize the configuration of his load, or to transport a non-conventional load such as a quartered game animal. Military packs are often external frame designs due to their ability to carry loads of different shapes, sizes and weights.

Internal Frame – This is a relatively recent innovation. An internal-frame pack has a large fabric section around an internal frame composed of strips of aluminum, titanium or plastic, sometimes with additional metal stays to reinforce the frame. A complex series of straps works with the frame to distribute the weight and hold it in place. The internal frame permits the pack to fit closely to the wearer's back and minimizes shifting of the load, which is desirable when participating in activities that involve upper-body movement such as scrambling over rocky surfaces or skiing. This tight fit reduces ventilation, resulting in these type of packs tend to be more sweaty than an external frame pack. The internal construction also allows for a large storage compartment; a few lash points may be present, but as the frame is completely integrated, it is difficult to securely lash larger and heavier items which do not fit inside the compartment to the outside of the pack. Internal frame packs originally suffered from smaller load capacity and less comfortable fit during steady walking, but newer models have improved greatly in these respects. In addition, because of their snug fit, the improved internal frame models have largely replaced external frame backpacks for many activities.

In my research, the best 72-Hour bag is one made for military purposes. The reason is because of the amount of testing and field research that has gone into it. However, your color choices are often limited to Camouflage, Olive (OD Green), Tan, and Black. While typically not the most beautiful bags, their utility and functionality is the main concern. Also the ability to blend in with surroundings makes these bags desirable with those who feel the art of camouflage may be needed.

CFP 90 Assault Pack

That being said there are a lot of commercial backpacks that offer some of the advantages that military bags offer, with an array of colors to choose from. So the bag you choose is obviously going to be determined by how much space you want or need and functionality.

Size is the next thing to consider when looking at a 72-Hour bag. Having the biggest size bag possible may not always be better. A reasonably sized 72-Hour bag will depend on how much you're able to carry so you will have to make that determination for yourself. The formula for pack weight is that it should not weigh more than a ¼ of your body weight. Those numbers can fluctuate based on your physical fitness and the type of terrain you will be moving through. A quick example is I weigh 220 pounds, so my actual max pack weight should be 45-55 pounds.

Most of the bags available have the ability to expand as well as to strap things to the outside so the weight that you're able to load onto it can vary considerably. Keep in mind that this all counts to your maximum pack weight.

One thing that you want to be very careful with when choosing the best 72-Hour bag for yourself is how much the bag itself weighs. Some bags can weigh up to several pounds and the weight of the bag can limit what you could carry in it. Most ideally there are bags that weigh less than 10 pounds and can adequately carry substantial amounts of gear. That is ideally what you want to look for when choosing your best 72-hour bag.

Straps and expendable compartments on the outside of the bag can increase substantially what can be carried and increase what you're able to take with you so that is something you will look at. It will give you the option to take more with you if it doesn't make your bag too heavy. It will also allow you to organize things better so that you don't have to dig to the bottom of your bag every time you need an item.

CHAPTER 4

THE BASICS

The basics of survival are Water, Food, Shelter, Fire, Health, and Attitude. I placed them in that order for a reason. That is their order of importance, you can have all the food you need but without water you're in trouble. Always remember the Rule of Three. You can survive - 3 minutes without air, 3 hours without a regulated body temperature, 3 days without water, and 3 weeks without food.

WATER

Water by far is going to be your most important resource. Since the human body is composed of up to 78% water, it should be no surprise that water is first and foremost on the list. Typically a person drinks almost a gallon of water per day. People in survival situations usually perish due to dehydration, or the debilitating effects of waterborne pathogens from untreated water. Dysentery can become deadly when not treated. Just because it looks clean doesn't mean it is clean.

FOOD

I place food higher on the list than most other people. Despite the fact that you can survive for much longer without it as compared with water. Three weeks without food, as opposed to three days without water. Your body uses calories for fuel and when you don't have food your body has to get those calories from somewhere else…your fat reserves. Studies have shown that the longer you go without food the less you are able to accomplish. The longer you go without food the less distance you will be able to travel. The faster your strength and endurance will be drained, and the longer it will take you to regain it back.

SHELTER

Many people when in survival situations often get into serious trouble due to direct exposure to the elements. Sadly a lot of people in survival situations die of hypothermia, which can be easily avoided. Being able to build a shelter is of importance when in a survival situation. It is also extremely important to minimize heat loss, and minimize water loss as well. I place shelter above fire because a shelter will protect you from the elements better than a fire ever will.

FIRE

Even though it is not usually considered a survival need, fire is one of the most useful things you need. It can help warm your body or your shelter, dry your clothes, boil your water, and cook your food. Fire also provides psychological support and creates a sense of security and safety.

Ideally, it is best to carry multiple fire-starting tools, such as a lighter, matches, and flint and steel. Good fire-making skills are invaluable. If you were to find yourself in a situation without a modern fire-making implement, fire by friction is the most effective primitive technique. Popular friction fire-making methods include bow drill, hand drill, fire plow, and fire saw.

HEALTH

Maintaining your health is paramount. Even minor injuries can affect the outcome of your survival. Having even a basic first aid kit can be useful in helping a person survive and function with injuries and illnesses that would otherwise kill or incapacitate them.

ATTITUDE

Attitude is by far one of the most important skills to have and the hardest one to achieve. The reason for this is that sometimes in a survival situation you may have to do something that goes against your personal beliefs. Attitude determines how successful you are in a survival situation. This basic survival skill might even determine whether you live or die. Some people simply call this "The will to live."

We will delve into each of these in greater depth in the following chapters.

CHAPTER 5

WATER

To maintain good health, the human body needs a minimum of two quarts of water per day. If you are in a survival situation, chances are you'll be exerting yourself, and you may be in a hot or cold environment. Both of these factors mean you will need to drink more than the minimum amount of water. It's easy to think that a cold environment is less of a risk, but that's not the case. While you may perspire less, you lose water through your skin because of the dry air. In heavy winds you should also drink more water. Any time you are perspiring you are also loosing water and need to replace it.

Your body is about two-thirds water and uses it to help circulate blood, process food and assist other internal processes. If you use more water than you take in, you will begin to suffer from dehydration. If this continues you will develop severe dehydration. This results in your cells shrinking and circulation slows and eventually stops, resulting in a lack of oxygen flow to your muscles. Eventually this will result in death. Dehydration can set in as soon as six hours without water, and more than a full day without water is cause for serious concern. The human body can only live about three days without water.

Now that we understand the importance of water, it should be pretty clear why it is number one priority. Water is going to be your single most important resource that you will need in a survival situation. One gallon of water weighs 8.34 pounds. Three gallons would be 25 pounds, or in my case half my maximum pack weight. If we consider that you are not going to be using it for anything else other than drinking. It is still unfeasible to think that you can pack and carry three to five gallons of water.

You will however want to make sure you have some water with you. There are several ways to carry water and many different types of canteens that you can purchase. I however like the functionality of the CamelBak® type systems. These usually consist of a bladder (usually 70 to 100oz.) with a long tube at the bottom and a bite valve on the other end. They come with a protective cover that you can either lash to your pack or has pack like straps on it. There are several companies that make similar type products so you do not necessarily have to buy a CamelBak® system.

CamelBak® Hotshot

They also come with a Molle style cover as well if you wish to strap it to the Molle straps on your pack. This is really a nice option if your Pack supports it.

CamelBak® Storm

It is true that 100 oz. of water will not be enough one person to last three days. A 100 oz. is equivalent to about ¾ of a gallon of water you are going to need to refill it eventually. If you're lucky enough to find a source, you need to make sure you can purify it. Clear rivers and lakes may look clean, but there are millions of organisms in fresh water. If you don't purify it, you can get extremely sick from bacteria or viruses. In a survival situation you should err on the side of caution. Never assume that a source is completely safe to drink from without purifying it first.

Purifying water can be done several ways, some more time

consuming than others. Obviously in a survival situation or in a situation where you need to keep moving you are not going to have the luxury of boiling water. While boiling water is the most effective method of purifying it. It requires a heat source and a vessel to hold the water. To make sure your water is completely purified you should bring the water to a rolling boil for three to five minutes to purify it.

When purifying your water, you will need to check whether it is cloudy first. Cloudy water needs to be filtered prior to boiling so you do not ingest the debris. To filter the water, you can use items like coffee filters, cloths, bandana, or even a sock (preferably clean) and pour the water through it. You should filter the water as many times as necessary until it becomes clear. Remember though this type of filtering does not remove or kill microscopic pathogens the water might contain.

There are a lot of products out on the market that can filter water. Many of these are simple hand pump systems that move water through a filter cartridge and discharge it out. These are very effective in removing Bacteria like Klebsiella, Giardia, and Cryptosporidium bacteria. As well as algae, spores, cysts, and other sediments. This is important because ingesting these can cause severe illness or death.

Using a filter pump

These filter pumps are generally very light weight and have replaceable filters. So it is best to carry one and a spare filter in your bag. Most filters are usually capacity rated to a max of 200 gallons (750 liters) depending on water quality. However some people say you can exceed these capacities a little bit and be fine. That is a risk I wouldn't want to take.

Katadyn® Hiker Pro Filter

Another type of filter system is The Lifestraw. Lifestraw is a portable filtration device that lets you safely drink directly from any fresh water source. It's about 11 inches long, less than 1 inch around, and looks like a jumbo drinking straw. One end has the narrow mouthpiece, the other goes directly into the water source. Each Lifestraw lasts 700 liters, roughly the amount of water needed for one person per year.

The filter gets rid of nearly 100 percent of waterborne bacteria, 98.7 percent of viruses and removes particles as small as 15 microns. It weighs only 140 grams and it just might make the difference in your chances of survival.

Lifestraw Water Filtration System

Even using a filter your water still might not be purified. While filters are a very good method for purifying water still won't remove viruses. Viruses such as Hepatitis A, Rotavirus, and Norwalk virus may still be in water after filtration. The only way to remove or neutralize things that might still be in the water after filtration is with chemical purification. There are two types of chemical treatment: those using iodine and those using chlorine. There are a number of products on the market, so you should follow the directions on the bottle. Be advised that many of the tablets have an expiration date and become ineffective after that point. Also, once the bottle has been opened, the tablets must be used within a certain period. When in doubt, buy a new bottle.

The effectiveness of all chemical treatment of water is related to the temperature, pH level, and clarity of the water. Cloudy water often requires higher concentrations of chemical to disinfect.

Add the chemical to the water and swish it around to aid in dissolving. Splash some of the water with the chemical onto the lid and the threads of the water bottle so that all water areas are treated.

The water should sit for at least 30 minutes after adding the chemical to allow purification to occur. If using tablets let the water sit for 30 minutes after the tablet has dissolved.

The colder the water, the less effective the chemical is as a purifying agent. Research has shown that at 50° F (10° C), only 90 percent of Giardia cysts were inactivated after 30 minutes of exposure. If the water temperature is below 40° F (4° C), double the treatment time before drinking. It is best if water is at least 60° F (16° C) before treating. You can place the water in the sun to warm it before treating.

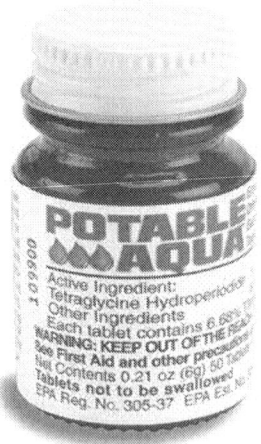

Portable Aqua Iodine Tablets

Chlorine can be used for persons with iodine allergies or restrictions. Remember that water temperature, sediment level, and contact time are all elements in killing microorganisms in the water. Remember to follow the manufacturer's instructions.

Portable Aqua Chlorine Tablets

Now that we have talked about how to purify your water now let us talk about where to find water. In a survival mode you need to not overlook any potential source of water. The most obvious sources are streams, rivers and lakes. But in an urban setting sinks and bath tubs can also be a good source. However if you're in an area after severe flooding you need to remember even that water can be contaminated. Water from a kiddie pool or dog bowl can become a viable source after purification. Even in extreme situations you can acquire water from mud puddles. Melting snow in the winter can also be used as a source of water. I have seen people pack flasks with snow and then place it in their coat to speed the melting process. If you are in an area where you are able to hunker down and can build a rain still this can be a viable water source. Even in extreme cases you can turn to water recycling. This is simply a matter of recapturing your own urine and consuming it. If you need to do this task remember to boil it first for 5 to 10 minutes before drinking. Remember to always treat any water that you find after an emergency situation as contaminated and to treat it accordingly.

CHAPTER 6

FOOD

You might be surprised to see food so high on my list of the basic survival skills priorities list. This is because in a survival situation you are going to need to keep moving. It takes a lot of energy to traverse terrain and to maintain your mental composure than most people realize. Being able to replace the protein your body uses is essential in survival situations. While we can survive for much longer without food as compared to water. Thankfully, most natural environments are filled with a variety of items that can meet our nutritional needs. Wild plants often provide the most readily available foods, though insects and small wild game can also support our dietary needs in a survival situation.

Food is important for your mental and emotional state, as well as a source of energy and to maintain a normal body temperature. It is essential to understand where to find food. In a survival situation, you have to take advantage of everything available to eat. Most wilderness areas are full of natural food, ranging from plants to insects. The food sources you can exploit are determined by the habitat you are in. Vary your diet to make sure you get the appropriate proportions of fat, protein, carbohydrates, minerals and vitamins.

Meat and fish are good sources of protein and fat and provide virtually everything a long-term survivor would need. However, at the first stage of a survival situation, plants are the most appropriate diet as plants are easily accessible and contain the necessary carbohydrates.

Depending of the time of the year you will almost always find edible plants, unless you are in the middle of an arid desert. Knowledge of only one or two wild edible plants can be of great help in your search for survival food. Dandelion roots are one example of an edible plant that can be found almost anywhere.

Your most vital nutritional needs in a survival situation are protein and fat. Most insects are rich in both. Turn off your cultural bias against eating insects. Edible bugs are very good survival food. While eating bugs may not sound appetizing. When you get hungry enough you can and will eat just about anything. Earthworms are a great source of protein.

Fish are a valuable food source. Therefore, if you are near a river or stream, fishing is an important alternative to obtain food. Having even a basic set of fish hooks and line can be all you need to successfully catch fish.

Unless you are an experienced hunter, hunting animals for meat is inadvisable in a survival situation. Hunting is difficult and you will expend a lot of energy to get your food. Instead of hunting consider trapping. Trapping requires less skill and leaves you free to spend time searching for other food sources. The wilderness survivor needs simple traps that are easy to remember and easy to construct. Eggs offer high nutritional value, are convenient and safe. They can be boiled, baked or fried. The first obvious place to look for them is a bird nest. However, not all birds build a nest, but instead lay their eggs directly on the ground or in a hole.

Cooking is a skill of great importance for all wilderness travelers. Cooking not only makes many foods more appetizing to taste, but also ensure that parasites and bacteria are killed. You don't want to get sick from food poisoning.

In your 72-Hour bag you will want to have at least a three day supply of food. Think conservative because canned food weighs more than freeze dried food.

Freeze-dried food and meals are very appealing both because of their weight and their variety. The creation of dehydrated foods is an ancient technique that has been used for millennia as a simple method of food storage for the long winter months. Removing the water from food greatly delays the development of mold or bacterial growth. This is why dehydrated food supplies to last much longer than fresh food would. The dehydrating process slowly removes water from the food using warm temperatures, making the food lighter in weight, smaller and resistant to decay. This makes dehydrated food perfect for long-term storage.

Mountain House Dehydrated Meals

The variety of dehydrated meals is quite vast. Dehydrated meals are light and due to their size you can pack and carry a considerable amount of them. The downside to dehydrated meals is that they require water to reconstitute and in a survival situation water conservation may be a priority. Some dehydrated meals like the Sausage Patty or the Ice Cream Bar can actually be eaten without reconstituting it. The disadvantage to this practice is it makes you thirsty and draws water from your body.

Another alternative and a personal choice of mine are the Meal, Ready-to-Eat, commonly known as the MRE. The MRE is a self-contained, individual field ration in lightweight packaging bought by the United States military for its service members for use in combat or other field conditions. You can find it for sale at most army surplus stores and at several retailers online.

The MRE is designed to provide complete nutrition and energy requirements for personnel in the field. MRE meals provide 1,250 calories and one-third of the day's recommended allowance of vitamins and minerals. Everything in the MRE is ready to eat; it does not require rehydration or even cooking necessary. Only the drink requires the addition of water. Each military MRE comes with a heater for optional warming of the entrée portion of the meal. Even condiments or seasonings and a biodegradable spoon are provided.

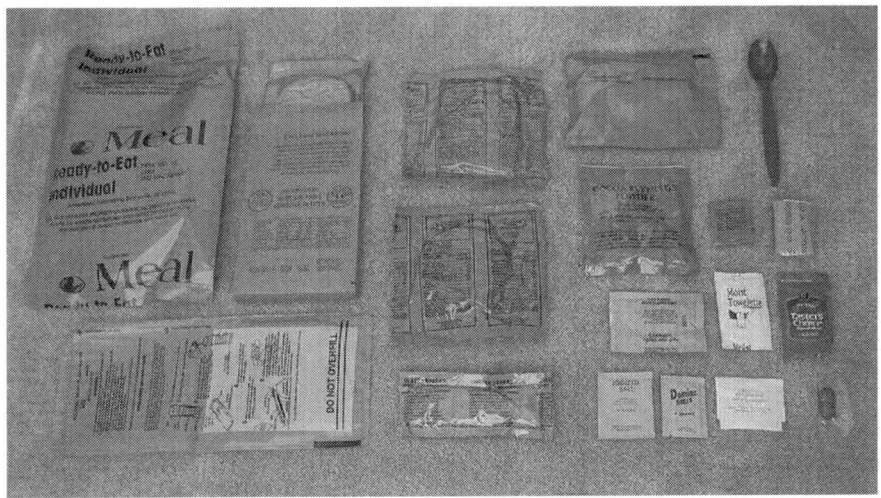

MRE with Heater

General contents may include:

Main course (entree)

Side dish

Dessert or snack (often commercial candy, or fortified pastry)

Crackers or bread

Spread of cheese, peanut butter, or jelly

Powdered beverage mix: (fruit flavored drink, cocoa, or coffee)

Utensils (usually just a plastic spoon)

Flameless ration heater (FRH)

Beverage mixing bag

Accessory pack:

Xylitol chewing gum

Water-resistant matchbook

Napkin / toilet paper

Moist towelette

Seasonings (salt, pepper, sugar, creamer, and/or Tabasco sauce)

MRE shelf life is estimated to be three years when stored at 80 degrees Fahrenheit. Special time-temperature indicators are on the cases, making it easy to tell when the MRE rations have expired. The indicators change based on the temperature of storage, so if kept well below 80 degrees, the MRE shelf life is lengthened.

Because MRE food is completely ready to eat, each meal is heavier than a corresponding Freeze Dried or Dehydrated meal. If you choose to go with Dehydrated, Freeze-dried, or MRE's always remember to rotate your meals and check for expired or spoiled meals. There is nothing worse than being in a survival situation and finding out that your food is not consumable.

CHAPTER 7

CLOTHING

Clothing is a priority item to consider. If you are forced to grab your bag and go you are probably going to only have the clothes on your back and the shoes on your feet. This is only going to get you so far and depending on the elements you may need to make a change in the clothing you are wearing very soon.

The following is a personal list of what I carry in my 72-Hour bag. You should consider this as a guideline and not a hard and fast rule. If you feel the need to carry something additional and you have the weight and the space to spare go for it.

Socks – 4 Pair (2-Pair Cotton, 2 Pair thermal) while cotton doesn't provide thermal protection it does breathe well, and is comfortable. Thermal socks are essential for colder climates. (Wool socks will provide thermal protection when wet and are always a good choice. I am also aware of the number of synthetic materials on the market such as Gore-Tex; this is a matter of preference.

Footwear – One pair of good quality hiking shoes or boots. In the event that you have to walk especially over long distances this will be essential. Walking overland in tennis shoes for miles will be murder on your feet. Hiking boots and shoes will provide better support for long treks that you may incur. My personal preference is the Merrell Moab GORE-TEX® XCR® they are waterproof and very comfortable.

Moab Gore-Tex XCR Mid

Pants – Two pairs of pants of your choice. Again try to think about lightweight and water resistant. The problem with jeans is once they get wet they get cold and cold will sap your strength quickly. Military BDU pants are a nice choice because they loose-fitting and allow ease of movement they also have cargo pockets which become useful. However there are several types out there to choose from.

Shirts – Two Shirts (One Long Sleeve, One Short sleeve) One T-shirt and one long sleeve shirt should be adequate for comfortably and protection. Thermal Long sleeve Henley's are always a good choice.

Jacket – One I prefer a layered jacket system that is one that has an outer shell that is waterproof and wind proof and can be worn alone or with a zip in thermal inner shell that can also be worn separately. This gives you essentially three jackets in one.

Columbia Jacket

Base layer - **3 pair** cotton underwear and one set (top and bottom) of thermal underwear. Preferably choose thermal base layer garments that wick moisture away from your body.

Headwear – Two (One baseball cap, or wide brim hat and one thermal beanie.) The baseball cap will be valuable to shade your eyes from the sun and will reduce eyestrain. A wide brim hat will do the same but will also keep sun off your ears and neck preventing these areas from getting sunburned. A thermal beanie will keep both your head and ears warm during cold nights and in lower temperatures.

Sunglasses – One pair these will become invaluable on hot sunny days as well as sunny winter days when the sun radiates of the snow.

Belt – A heavy duty belt such as a "Last Chance Belt" or a nylon or leather duty belt is ideal.

Miscellaneous – I always find it handy to carry few bandanas with you as well. They are very useful they can be used to filter water, as a simple bandage, or to cover your mouth and nose in dust storms.

Clothing is nothing you should scrimp on. You want to find clothing that is comfortable and will meet the needs you expect to find yourself in. Keep in mind that you may be wearing these clothes for several days, maybe even weeks.

One other important thing to remember about clothing is that it is always a smart idea to layer clothing when possible to conserve body heat. However also remember to remove layers if you start to perspire. When you perspire you start losing water. Conserving water is always a major concern when you are in a survival situation.

CHAPTER 8

SHELTER

Many people who are forced into survival situations often get into serious trouble because of direct exposure to the elements. Most people in survival situations die of hypothermia, which can be easily avoided with basic survival skills. Being able to build a shelter is of paramount importance in a survival situation. It is extremely important to prevent or minimize heat loss, or if in a desert environment, to minimize water loss.

There are many types of shelters to consider including natural shelters such as caves, hollow stumps and logs, as well as building shelters such as a debris hut, lean-to, debris tipi, scout pit or snow shelter. When considering your 72-Hour bag needs shelter should be of utmost concern. A tent would be the ideal item to consider. In the event that you don't have the luxury of a tent a tarp can also be used to make a general shelter. Tents range in size from "bivouac" structures, just big enough for one person to sleep in, up to tents big enough to sleep ten people. When considering a tent you need to keep a few things in mind.

1. How many people will need to stay in the tent.

2. Will you store gear inside the tent or outside.

3. What environmental elements will the tent need to protect you against.

A general three season tent will suffice for most people and even though technically they are not rated for winter applications they will keep you dry and out of the elements. Even if you are considering just a tent for yourself you always need to consider weight. One-person tents range between 2 and 3 pounds. Two-person tents commonly range from 3 to 5 pounds. When looking for a tent you want to aim for a per-person weight of less than 3 pounds (less is always better). Realize, though, that a low per-person weight usually results in a snug interior.

Mountaineering or Expedition tents are more suited to winter camping, but weigh considerably more and cost more. With a three-season tent and a tarp you can create a substantial shelter that will keep you well protected in the winter months. When choosing a tent take your time and research as much as possible and then go try out different models you are considering. Most outdoor stores set up tents for display in the spring this is the best time to go out and test them, lay down and make sure you are comfortable in them. Nothing is worse than finding out your new tent is not big enough for you to lie down in comfortably.

A tarp can also be an effective shelter. With a couple stakes and two poles you can make an A-frame tent. The disadvantage to this is that you usually end up lying on the cold ground. If you carry a second tarp you can use it as a floor. However this is added weight.

Tarp Shelter

Sleeping gear is the next thing to think about. A good sleeping bag can make the difference between getting much needed rest and comfort, or spending a night shivering to death. As with everything else this will be a matter of preference as there are several options in which one can take when looking at sleeping systems.

One option is a Cowboy Bed Roll these are usually favored because they are lightweight and can also double to hold other items. A Cowboy Bed Roll is comprised of a cotton duck canvas. The canvas is very rugged and water resistant. Inside you can have a foam mattress a couple blankets and sheets, or just a sleeping bag. They usually have a flap to pull over your head and keep you dry as well.

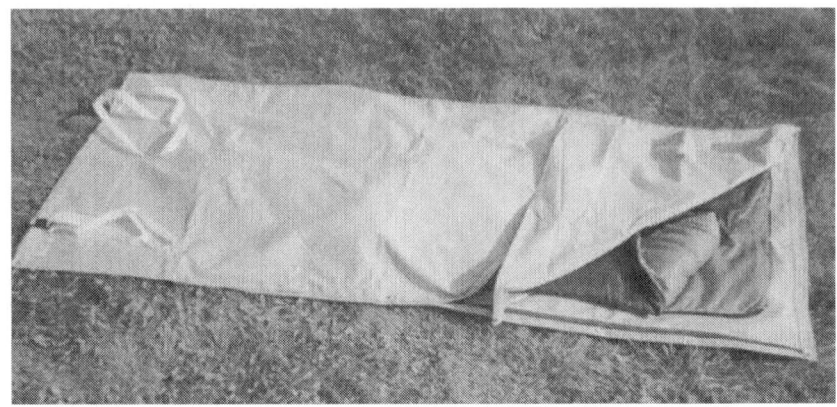

Cowboy Bed Roll

Another option is a general use sleeping bag. There are several out on the market each with different features and temperature ratings.

The Modular Sleep System (MSS) is a modular sleeping bag used by the United States armed forces.

The MSS consists of a camouflaged, waterproof, breathable Gore-Tex cover, a lightweight patrol sleeping bag, and an intermediate cold weather sleeping bag. Compression sacks are included to store and carry the system. The MSS is available in colors compatible with the universal camouflage pattern. The patrol bag provides cold weather protection from 35 to 50 degrees Fahrenheit. The intermediate bag provides cold weather protection from minus 5 to 35 degrees Fahrenheit. Together, the patrol bag and intermediate bags provide extreme cold weather protection in temperatures as low as minus 30 degrees Fahrenheit. The cover can be used with each of three MSS configurations (patrol, intermediate, or combined) to be comparable with the environment in which the system is being used; the cover provides environmental protection from wind and water.

The sleeping bags are made of rip-stop nylon fabrics and continuous filament polyester insulation; camouflage cover is made with waterproof, breathable Gore-Tex. The compression sack is made with water-resistant, durable nylon fabric.

Modular Sleep System

Personally I prefer the MSS to a normal sleeping bag since I change my bag with the seasons I can take out the heavier intermediate bag during spring summer and fall months and put it in during the winter months. Also the camouflage cover while not ideal can double as a makeshift shelter in place of a tent when needed.

CHAPTER 9

FIRE

Even though it is not commonly a survival need. Fire is one of the most useful basic survival skills you can master. Fire is useful for keeping yourself or your shelter warm, drying out your clothes and shoes, boiling your water, and cooking your food. Fire also provides psychological support in survival situations by creating a sense of security and safety. Fire can also be used as signaling device. At night the light from a camp fire can be seen from up to a mile away. This distance increases depending on the size of the fire as well. During the day you can burn certain items to create smoke that can also be used to signal people. The down side is that if you are trying to avoid being found a fire is not practical. Lastly a fire will also be effective for keeping critters away from your camp.

Ideally, when traveling in the wilderness, it is best to carry multiple fire-starting tools, such as a lighter, matches, flint and steel, etc... Popular friction fire-making methods include bow drill, hand drill, fire plow, and fire saw. Even with these implements starting a fire can be challenging in inclement weather. Sometimes starting a fire in perfect conditions can be just as challenging. I highly recommend practicing fire starting in different weather conditions within different habitats. Practicing several different types of fire making techniques will be beneficial when in a situation where one method may not be working.

The most popular friction fire making method is the Bow Drill. The benefit to the bow drill is that you can find materials almost anywhere in the wild and don't have to carry a kit with you. All you need is a knife and string or shoelace.

There are places you can purchase a Bow Drill kit. They are of very good quality and well made. You can also usually find the materials in the wild to make a Bow Drill kit as well.

There are five parts to the bow-drill set. The bow, the string, the spindle/drill, the board, and the handhold. The drill spins against the board on one end and is held vertically by the handhold at the other end. The drill is spun by the bow and string.

The Board:

The board should be about three inches wide, and an inch thick. And relatively flat on both sides if possible.

The Spindle:

This should be about a foot-long straight-grained section of wood. It should be slightly less than a one-inch diameter straight dowel. Whittle the last inch of each end into sharp points.

The Handhold:

This is a section approximately four to five inches long. Whittle down the edges to remove any rough spots and to provide a comfortable surface for gripping. On the flat side in the center is a hole.

The String:

There are a wide variety of materials strings can be made of. In general, use a string that is at least one and a half times the length of your bow. The string should be relatively thick. A thickness of a quarter-inch will last a long time. Shoelaces are usually not thick enough for repeated use but in a pinch can be used. It is best to avoid synthetics such as nylon as they sometimes melt from the friction.

The Bow:

Find a section of a green (live) branch that is about the thickness of your index finger and almost straight or slightly curved and the length of your arm from elbow to fingertip. The bow should be reasonably flexible but not flimsy.

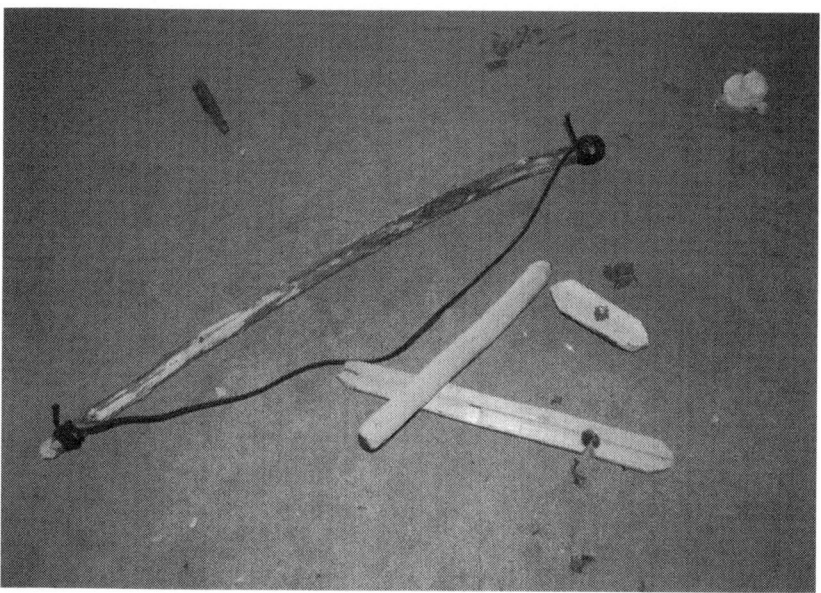

Bow Drill Set

Using the Bow Drill:

If you are right-handed, hold the bow with this hand. Place the board flat on the ground so it is stable. Take your spindle and push the point into the board so that you make a mark. This mark should be about one inch from the edge of the board. It should also be at one end of the board so that you have room to place your foot. The bow is tilted slightly down to avoid rubbing the string against itself.

Put your left foot on the board (if you are right-handed) so the inside ball of your foot is next to the shallow gouge. Your right knee should be on the ground and you should be sitting on your right foot. Your right leg should be parallel to the board.

Load the spindle by wrapping the string around the spindle so that the spindle is outside of the bow. The spindle should feel like it's going to pop out. The tighter the string is, the better, just don't make it so tight that it breaks the bow. Holding the loaded spindle and bow in your right hand, place the bottom point of the spindle into the hole in the board. Cap the other end with the handhold and apply some pressure to keep the spindle from popping out.

Simply begin stroking the bow back and forth slowly. Keep the pressure on the handhold fairly high. Eventually, you should see a small amount a smoke forming at one or both ends of the spindle. Pick up a little bit of speed until both ends are smoking. Continue until you generate an ember that you can transfer to a tinder bundle.

This is a very simple explanation that takes a lot of practice to learn how to do it effectively and properly.

Using a Bow Drill

Lighters, matches, and flint and steel are other options that are quick and easy and lightweight. The problem with lighters is they need to be filled with lighter fluid and that can leak out or evaporate over time. Personally I don't recommend relying on a lighter for fire making in any survival situation. You can find Waterproof, Windproof, or Stormproof matches in any outdoor store or online retailer. They are often expensive and in my experience rarely work. I used one set that said they were waterproof. My experience with them was that I couldn't light it when it got wet, wouldn't light dry and still didn't light when I threw it into the fire. My solution is to purchase a good quality waterproof match case and fill it with regular wood matches. A good quality case will keep them dry and ready for use whenever you need them.

Waterproof Match Case

The other option is flint and steel. Flint and steel igniters work in any environment. They are designed to start fires in any weather, and at any altitude. Despite getting wet, a flint and steel will create a 5,500-degree F spark that will light relatively dry tinder. This is an advantage over relying on matches and lighters, as they will not function when wet. Another solution is Magnesium and steel similar to a flint and steel except that it incorporates a small block of magnesium that you shave some off and surround it with your tinder and then use the flint and steel striker to ignite the magnesium that lights the tinder.

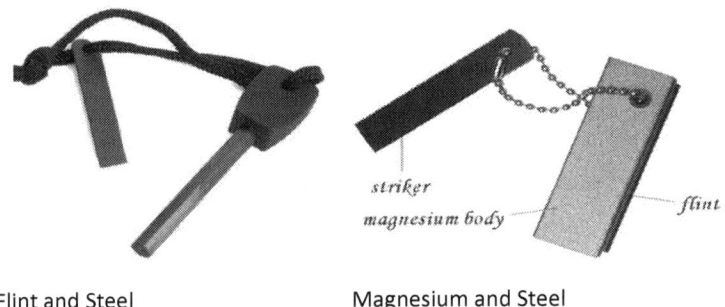

striker

magnesium body

flint

Flint and Steel   Magnesium and Steel

Tinder is the next thing to consider when building a fire. Most people instantly think that tinder is just small twigs and sticks. While it is it really makes poor tinder. Tinder should burn easily and be abundantly available. Common materials used as tinder are.

- Dry pine needles, leaves or grass
- Birch bark
- Cloth, lint, or frayed rope
- Cotton Balls, cotton swabs, tampons
- Paper, paper towels, toilet paper
- Shoe polish
- Charred wood
- Some types of fungus
- Bird down
- Small twigs
- Pine Tar or Pitch

Personally I like to carry a small zip close bag with ten to fifteen cotton balls in it to use as tinder. I have also heard of other people doing the same thing but also adding alcohol, lighter fluid, or Vaseline to the bag to saturate the cotton balls. This is a practice I am not comfortable in using but others may. I find that my cotton balls tend to ignite just fine being dry.

Finally I will add one last item to consider. Sterno Fuel is a jellied petroleum product, is an excellent source of cooking fuel. Sterno is very lightweight, odorless, and can be easily ignited with a match or a spark from flint and steel. It is not explosive and it's safe for use indoors. There are also things such as Fire Paste that are similar to Sterno. These are great for starting fires and will ignite even if wet. They are lightweight and easily carried. On more than one occasion I have started a fire by taking a small amount of Sterno out of a can and placing it on top of my kindling and igniting it.

The disadvantage of Sterno is that it will evaporate very easily, even when the lid is securely fastened. If you store Sterno, you should check it every six to eight months to ensure that it has not evaporated beyond the point of usage.

Sterno Fuel

Fire Paste

Fire Paste is another gel type fire starter. It works similar to Sterno as in touching flame or spark to it and it will burn, but it does have its limitations. It will not ignite wet tinder unless you use a large amount; even then it is a tricky thing to accomplish. Some people have even gone as far as making homemade napalm. Due to safety considerations I will discuss that any further.

CHAPTER 10

HEALTH

Maintaining your health is going to be paramount in any survival situation. In most events you are going to want to have at least a basic First Aid Kit. Keep in mind that you are solely responsible for your ultimate health and wellness in any survival situation. That being said you need to keep a few things in mind. First we will look at things that can kill you without you realizing it. First is avoiding dehydration. Dehydration results from inadequate replacement of lost body fluids. It decreases your efficiency, and if injured, it can increase your susceptibility to severe shock. Even a 5% loss of body fluids can result in nausea, and weakness. It is estimated that you are already 2% dehydrated before you crave fluids or feel thirsty.

The most common signs and symptoms of dehydration:

Dark urine with a very strong odor.

Low urine output.

Dark, sunken eyes.

Fatigue.

Emotional instability.

Loss of skin elasticity.

Delayed capillary refill in fingernail beds.

Trench line down center of tongue.

A loss of greater than 15% of body fluids may result in death. It is very important that you monitor fluid intake and fluid loss as well. Even though you lose water through respiration and other normal bodily functions the main one to be concerned with here is perspiration. When your body sweats you are losing precious water. The moment you realize you are starting to sweat you need to stop and remove clothing. Taking off a jacket will allow your body to cool off and save bodily water by not having to perspire to cool it. Managing perspiration is just as important in the winter as it is in the summer months.

Another concern is hypothermia, Hypothermia is a condition in which core body temperature drops below the required temperature for normal metabolism and body functions which is defined as 95.0 °F. Body temperature is usually maintained near a constant level of 98–100 °F through biologic homeostasis or thermoregulation. When your body is exposed to cold and its internal mechanisms are unable to replenish the heat that is being lost, a drop in core temperature occurs. As body temperature decreases, characteristic symptoms occur such as shivering and mental confusion. Hypothermia can be prolonged or can happen rather quickly; mental confusion is often the last stage prior to death. The key characteristic in hypothermia is shivering. As your body starts to shiver you are in a mild stage of hypothermia. Your body is attempting to warm itself by causing you to shiver. As you move into moderate stage of hypothermia shivering will become more violent, often incorporating the entire body. And muscle mis-coordination occurs. As you move into the severe stage of hypothermia shivering often stops and severe confusion sets in. It is at this stage that death usually occurs.

Other cold-related injuries that you need to look out for are Frostbite this is the freezing and destruction of tissue. Typically happens to exposed extremities. Frostnip is a superficial cooling of tissues without cellular destruction. And trench foot due to repetitive exposure to wet, non-freezing temperatures

Another concern is going to be foot problems. To prevent serious foot problems, break in your shoes before wearing them. Wash and massage your feet daily. Trim your toenails straight across. Wear an insole and the proper size of dry socks. Check your feet daily for blisters.

If you get a small blister, do not open it. An intact blister is safe from infection. Apply a padding material around the blister to relieve pressure and reduce friction. If the blister bursts, treat it as an open wound. Clean and dress it daily and pad around it. Leave large blisters intact.

I personally love the product called moleskin. In the case of a blister, the moleskin is cut with a hole in the center so the fabric does not adhere to the blister directly. The thickness of the surrounding moleskin protects the blister from further friction.

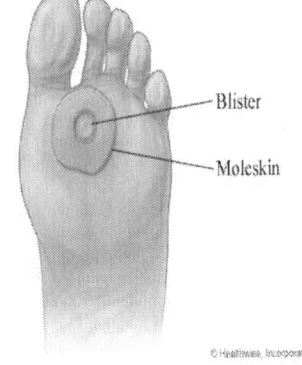

Moleskin   Moleskin Blister

To avoid having the blister burst or tear under pressure and cause a painful and open sore, do the following.

Obtain a sewing-type needle and a clean or sterilized thread. Run the needle and thread through the blister after cleaning the blister. Detach the needle and leave both ends of the thread hanging out of the blister. The thread will absorb the liquid inside. This reduces the size of the hole and ensures that the hole does not close up.

A second method is to use a needle to puncture the blister and gently squeeze the fluid out. Once you have removed all the fluid and it is now flat pad the entire area with moleskin.

Your basic First Aid kit should contain the following:

3 individually sealed gauze rolls

2 suture needles with thread

10 suture wound closing strips (Butterfly Strips)

2 Thin Cinch Universal trauma dressing

5 4x4 bandages

1 roll cloth tape

2 ACE bandages

1 SAM splint

1 CPR mask

1 pair scissors

1 pair of Tweezers

5 packs Water Gel pain relief gel for burns.

Several Band-Aids of various sizes

4 Moleskin sheets

Aloe Vera gel

10 Iodine tablets for wound disinfecting

Thermometer

Imodium or Pepto-Bismol pills

Tylenol

Benadryl tablets

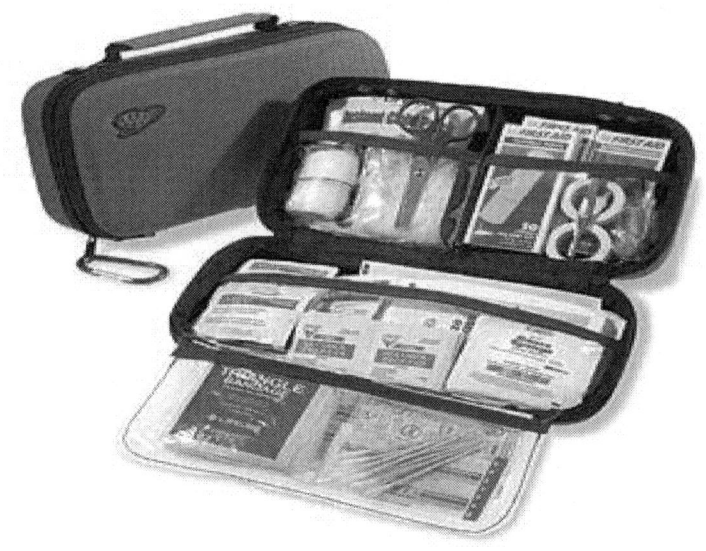

First Aid Kit

You can find a First Aid kit almost anywhere and most basic First Aid kits will contain most of the items I listed. You can also find First Aid kit bags and then choose to fill them with whatever you feel is necessary. When considering health needs for a 72-Hour bag you will want to consider medications you take on a regular basis. This would include prescription drugs that you can't or should not go without. If you take something on a daily basis it should be in your drug kit. When I use the term drug kit I mean prescription medicines that you need to take daily. High blood pressure meds, thyroid medications, etc… should all be in a separate drug kit. As with everything else you can always go for a bigger kit if you prefer, remember that bigger often means more weight. You may also consider taking a couple of what if items. I suggest that everybody at least carry one or two packets of QuikClot. QuikClot is a gauze bonded with kaolin it causes the coagulation of blood. It is typically used to slow or stop severe bleeding. The dressings can be left in place for up to 24 hours. However if you are in a position where you need to use a QuikClot product, follow up hospital care will most likely be needed.

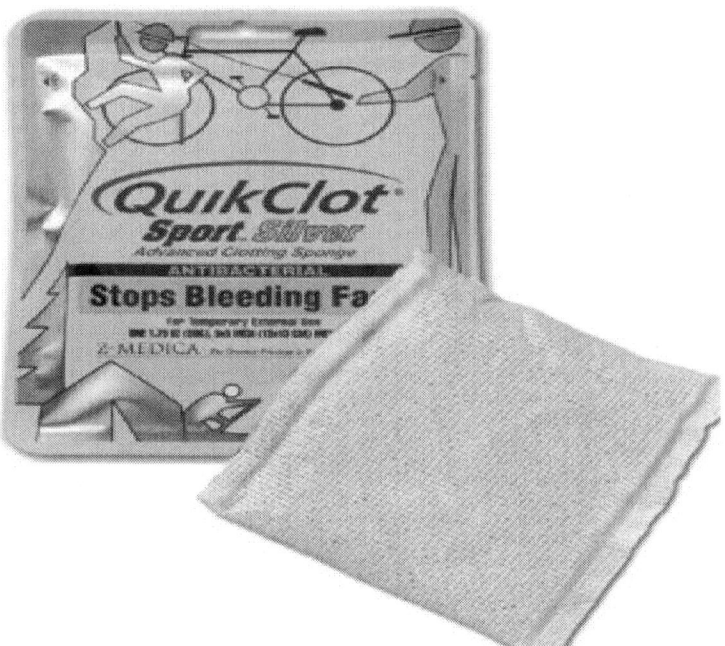

QuikClot

CHAPTER 11

ATTITUDE

More than any other skill, your attitude determines how successful you are in a survival situation. This basic survival skill might even determine whether you live or die. Surviving a difficult situation also requires meeting many challenges while avoiding panic and fear. When faced with a potential survival situation, remember the acronym SPEAR.

Stop

Plan

Execute

Assess

Re-evaluate

By systematically assessing, planning, and executing your basic survival skills, you will help keep your mind and body actively engaged in addressing your situation. This will greatly aid in avoiding panic, fear, and other negative states of mind. By maintaining an appropriate attitude, your chances of survival are greatly increased.

Attitude is by far one of the most important skills to have and the hardest one to achieve. The reason for this is that sometimes in a survival situation you may have to do something that goes against your personal beliefs. There is a thing I like to call the survival mindset. It usually kicks in with in the first few moments of fear when you realize that you are the only thing that you can depend on to get you through this.

I say fear because that first moment you realize that you are in a situation is frightening. Often referred to as the "Oh Shit" moment it is extremely frightening. That's why it is important to implement SPEAR as quickly as possible. Every time I have faced that "Oh Shit" moment I won't lie it has scared me. However by remaining calm and stopping to assess my surroundings and make an informed plan of action. Mitigating that fear is essential to maintaining control over the situation.

Although survival kits that contain some food, water, a first-aid kit, and some means of making fire are great to have on hand. It is important to remember that this is just a tool. The most important thing is having the right attitude. Here are some tips for productive ways to think that can assist you when disaster strikes.

Survival depends a great deal on a person's ability to withstand stress in emergency situations. Survival more often depends on the individual's reactions to stress than upon the danger, terrain, or nature of the emergency. To adapt is to live. Mental skills are much more important than physical skills in survival situations. A person's psychological reactions to the stress of survival can often make them unable to utilize their available resources.

One definitely must be in the proper frame of mind to survive an unplanned survival situation. Attitude or psychological state is most certainly number one. It is undoubtedly the most important ingredient of survival. With the proper attitude almost anything is possible. To make it through the worst a strong will or determination to live is needed. A powerful desire to continue living is a must. Without the will to live survival is impossible.

A positive attitude has a very strong influence on the mentality and motivation necessary. While in your survival situation you will be confronted with many problems that you will need to overcome. Your brain will be your best asset but it could also be your most dangerous enemy. You will have to defeat negative thoughts and imaginations, and also control and master your fears. You will need to shift mental processes and adopt that positive and optimistic can do attitude. Don't add any extra burden to yourself by falling into a destructive mental state like feeling self-pity or hopelessness.

Loneliness is a survival enemy that can hit you without warning. It will strike you when you realize you are the only person around who you can depend on while in your situation. Fight loneliness by keeping busy, singing, whistling, daydreaming, gathering food, or doing anything else that will take your mind off the fact that you are alone. Once again keep busy to keep your mind occupied. A deck of cards and a game of Solitaire can be a great loneliness breaker.

Fear is a big enemy to guard against. Fear is a completely normal reaction for anyone faced with an out of ordinary situation that threatens his important needs. There is no way to tell how someone will react to fear. Fear usually depends entirely on the individual rather than on the situation at hand. Fear could lead a person to panic or stimulate a greater effort to survive. Do your very best to control your fears. Expect fear and learn to recognize it. Control fear, don't let it control you. Fears can be lessened by keeping the body busy and free from thirst, hunger, pain, discomfort, and any other enemies to survival.

A more dangerous enemy than fear is panic. Panic is an uncontrolled urge to run or hurry from the situation. Panic is triggered by the mind and imagination under stress. It results from fear of the unknown, lack of confidence, not knowing what to do next, and a vivid imagination. Fear can build up to panic and cause a person to make a bad situation worse. In a panic a person's rational thinking disappears and can produce a situation that results in tragedy. To combat fear and panic keep your cool, relax, see the brighter side of things, and stay in control.

Keeping a positive mental outlook is for certain the most important aspect of survival. When you first realize that you're in a survival situation stop and regain your composure. Control your fears. Recognize dangers to your life. Relax and think; don't make any hasty judgments. Observe the resources around you. Analyze your situation and plan a course of action only after considering all of the aspects of your predicament. Be sure to keep cool and collected. It is important to make the right decision at all times. Set your goal of survival and always keep it fresh in your mind. Never give up. Prepare for the worst but hope for the best.

Believe that you can do something to make a difference in the situation. If people believe that life happens to them and they can't do anything about it, they won't do anything at all. Believe in yourself and your ability to take action, and your chances for survival are much higher.

I stated earlier that in a survival situation you may have to do something that is outside of your comfort range or against your personal beliefs. This may be minor like eating grubs and insects all the way to the extreme like killing something. Your personal survival should be your top priority. There is always the possibility that those that are unprepared when a situation arises will resort to stealing from those that are prepared. Maintaining personal security may become paramount to your survival. As a result you may need to take another's life for the sake of preserving your own. This would be a hard thing for anyone to do, however it may become necessary.

CHAPTER 12

PERSONAL PROTECTION

The idea of personal protection should be obvious to anyone considering a 72-Hour Bag. The idea that there are things out there that **can** and (if given the opportunity) **will** kill you should always factor into your preparations. Personal protection and security should be part of your 72-Hour Bag contents. Now first off let me state that I am not a proponent of violence. However in certain cases I can see where it could be used to ensure one's personal safety and security.

The very first item you need to develop is what is often referred to as Situational Awareness (SA). Situational Awareness is being aware of what is happening in the vicinity, in order to understand how information, events, and one's own actions will impact goals and objectives, both immediately and in the near future. When developing your own SA you need to understand the limits of your abilities and understand how they can change the situation at hand.

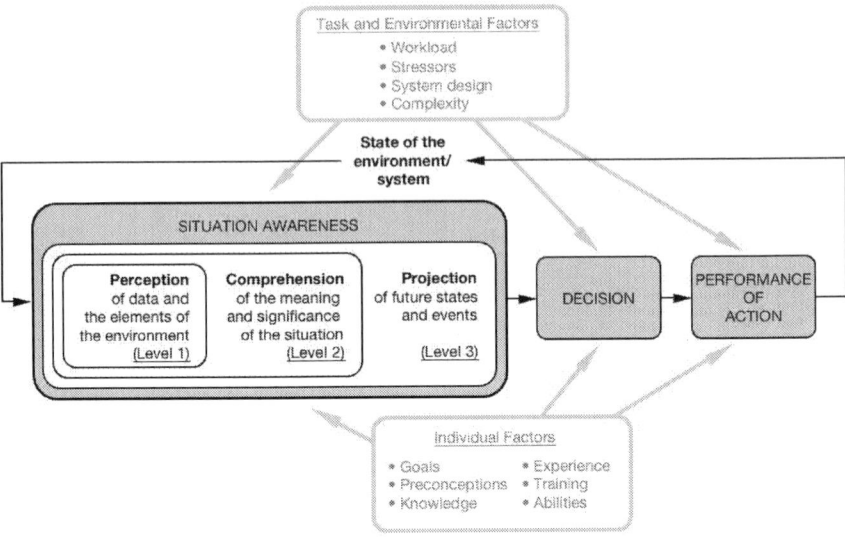

SA Model

Let us consider this hypothetical scenario. There is a severe breakdown in the fuel delivery system. As a result people are running out of gasoline and food supplies. This results in wide spread chaos. Since you live in a populated urban area people are resorting to looting and mob rule. All the stores are ransacked and empty. Running out of food you decide that it is time to leave for another locale.

Using SA you will be able to make informed decisions to make a plan. Should you leave at night or during the day? Do you go overland or do you go on established roads? Once you make a decision you need to consider how that choice will affect your ongoing SA. If you decide to go on established roads you may run the risk of running into a band of looters. If you choose to go overland and at night you may get injured on rough terrain and need medical attention.

Granted while this is a very crude overview to SA, it is effective at demonstrating the ideas and process. Every choice you make will have its pros and cons. Weighing those pros and cons and deciding which ones you can better mitigate is really what SA and surviving is all about. Unfortunately as anyone can tell you no plan ever goes 100% according to the plan.

Personal protection is the next thing you need to think about. Once you enter into a survival situation your number one priority should be personal safety. As with everything else when you consider personal safety equipment weight will be a factor. You should also consider items that will serve more than one purpose. Look for items that you will also be able to use effectively. Below are a few of my personal favorites and I will go into detail with each.

SOG Tactical Tomahawk

The SOG Tactical Tomahawk is a very versatile and useful tool. It can be used as an axe to cut kindling for starting fires, or to clear small trees and branches. It can be used as a hammer to pound tent pegs or nails. It has a spike on one end can be useful in breaching through walls and windows. It is lightweight at 24 ounces, and can be attached easily to a pack.

Gerber Prodigy Tanto

Knives are essential tools they can be used to open cans, gut fish, and cut large pieces of meat. They are also easily concealable, allowing you to carry several of them. I prefer to have on attached to my pack strap as well as carry one in my boot and on my belt. To some this may sound excessive but I have found on a number of occasions that a sharp knife is indispensable.

For most people at least a gun or two with ammunition is one of the other things that you might want to consider loading into your 72-Hour bag. It can serve as a deterrent as well as protection. The fact is during a situation you will need to be ready to deal with "no rule of law" when unpleasant stuff can happen. You need to be ready and able to take care yourself. The easiest way is with some kind of firearm.

I am well aware that it is a controversial subject but one you need to think through for yourself. There is an old saying, "desperate times call for desperate measures" and when times get desperate you will want to be able to protect yourself and your supplies. If someone can overpower you and take what you have, then your 72-Hour bag won't be very helpful.

Since we are talking guns I will lay out my personal preference and reasons behind it. First off when considering a firearm take into consideration the availability of ammunition. That really neat Smith & Wesson 41 caliber hand gun is nice, but 41 caliber ammunition is scarce. However calibers such as 9mm and 40 caliber are easily found in large quantities. And in scavenge situations it will be easier to find common ammunition than scarce ammunition.

Rifles are heavy and their ammunition is heavy as well. I am not suggesting that you not consider taking a rifle or shotgun. If that is your preference than go for it. You will need to consider its weight and how you will carry it. Handguns however are lighter by comparison and easier to carry. While handguns do not have the same effective range as a rifle they are still very useful. If you have to survive for a prolonged period of time you can bring down animals with a hand gun just as effectively as you can with a rifle.

Ideally the best option would be to take one or two handguns.

Preferably you would want them to be of the same caliber, since you will only want to carry one type of ammunition. You will want to carry enough ammunition. What is enough ammunition? You may be asking. That depends on your own preference. Again consider the weight of the ammunition as being part of your overall carrying weight. My personal preference would be 100 rounds. As a rule I always carry three magazines or clips for each gun. One in the gun at all times, and two extras loaded and ready to go. My pistol of choice holds 15 rounds so two extra clips equate to 45 rounds total before reloading. In any situation 15 rounds should be sufficient. If you find yourself in a situation where you are changing to your second clip; that should be the time you transition from fight mode to flight mode. Keep in mind that you always want to have all your clips for your gun (as well as your gun) within reach at all times.

There are several ways to carry a handgun with you. Hip holsters are usually the most common but are often problematic when using a backpack. Shoulder holsters are another nice option and add the ability to conceal it under a coat. Tactical or Drop Leg holsters are another good option for a couple of reasons. First it is a secure platform that allows it to move as part of your body. Second it positions the handgun in a natural drawing position. When worn correctly your arm should hang at your side naturally and your palm should rest against the grip of your handgun. Third it allows you to attach additional items to the holster assembly. Such as extra clip pouches, knife pouches, flashlights, and multi tool pouches.

Blackhawk Tactical Holster

There are a few other guidelines to consider when choosing to carry a firearm with you. First never leave a magazine or clip empty. If you find that you have spent all your ammunition and have changed to a new clip. At your earliest opportunity you should reload that clip. Second if you choose to carry a firearm you better know how to use it. Third never point the firearm at anything you don't intend to kill. Fourth and finally you need to carry a cleaning kit for it as well. I can't stress this point enough the military has a saying "A clean weapon can mean the difference between life and death." A clean and maintained weapon will rarely jam, misfire or malfunction.

Other items such as swords, machetes, crossbows, and bow and arrows can also be useful items as well. But again always consider how you are going to carry it and know how to effectively use them.

CHAPTER 13

MISCELLANEOUS

There are several items that you will also want to carry in your 72-Hour bag that don't fit in what we have already talked about. I have decided to include them in this chapter. Up to this point I have covered the basics for survival and ideally this will comprise at least 65 percent of your 72-Hour bag. However there are a still several items that you will want to have in your bag.

Midland's ER102 Emergency Crank Radio

Hand Crank Radio – these come in handy surprisingly more than one may think. They are small, lightweight, and often are filled with features. Ideally what you want is one that incorporates AM/FM radio, NOAA Weather channels, and offers both rechargeable battery and alkaline battery as well. Additional features like a flashlight, alarm clock, and USB port can also be useful. While the hand crank is useful for charging the flashlight or power the internal battery for the radio. It will take approximately 5 hours of straight cranking to charge a cell phone to 50%.

Binoculars – A lightweight pair of binoculars will also be useful not only for surveying the area around you but for also scouting out routes and terrain.

Flashlight/Glow Sticks – Kind of self-explanatory but become essential if you are going to be traveling at night. A head lamp will help you keep your hands free and have amazing battery life. Look for lights that use a LED bulb these tend to have the greatest battery life to burn ratio. Glow Sticks are another alternative and are great for in camp or used for marking other party members in the dark. But they tend to not produce enough light for trail walking or overland trekking. However they are lightweight and can be carried in large quantities.

Compass/GPS – GPS units are great and barring a complete failure of the satellite network very useful. However just like all electronic equipment it is dependent on battery power. The benefits of a compass are that it is easy to use, lightweight and error free. In no way do I discourage using a GPS. If you choose to be sure that you carry a compass and know how to use both.

Whistle and Signal Mirror – This may seem like a unusual item however they can draw a lot of attention from a great distance and are extremely lightweight. They can also be used to scare off animals that you encounter while on your own. Signal mirrors are another small lightweight item that can become invaluable when you need help and need to draw attention to yourself.

Goal Zero Nomad 7

Solar Panel Charger – Since you will undoubtedly carry an electronic device or two with you this should definitely on your list there are several types out there to choose from. Some even come with a rechargeable battery pack so you can recharge your rechargeable batteries. The nice advantage to a solar panel charger is you can usually attach it to your pack and recharge your devices or batteries while you are trekking through the environment.

Deck of Cards – A deck of cards or a paperback book or two or both. This is often overlooked but you must consider that a there can be large portions of your time to fill while you're either resting or waiting for help. Both a deck of cards and paperback books are light and take up very little space.

Mess Kit – A mess kit with a plate, eating utensil and something to cook on will be nice and invaluable. A titanium spork that incorporates a knife, fork and spoon into one device, is an effective eating utensil. A mess Kit should be lightweight and include a pot to boil water and a pan to cook with. A cup that can also be used to warm water will also be nice to have as well.

Fishing Kit – A small fishing kit that contains some hooks, weights, and fishing line. For obvious reasons these tools can become very valuable. It then would be easy to make a fishing pole and in turn possibly feed yourself. A small ice fishing pole can take up very little space and is easier than trying to make a pole.

Spice Kit – A spice kit is exactly what it sounds like. A bag that contains Iodized Salt, Pepper, and a couple other spices of choice. This becomes valuable when cooking fish or other items during survival situations.

Document Pack – Copies of important documents that you will need. Such as Driver's License, Passport, Birth Certificate, Social Security Cards, Marriage License, College Transcripts, Professional Certifications, Insurance Policies, etc. Notice that I said copies; I strongly believe that original documents should be kept in a safe and secure location.

Bartering Kit - Bartering with others while the infrastructure of an area is in shambles can be a very important aspect of survival.

Having things to trade like cash, precious metals (Gold and Silver), or even alcohol can be invaluable during these times.

Multi-tool – A multi-tool is a great idea to carry with you. For obvious reasons you will undoubtedly find it indispensable.

Rope/Para Cord – A length of utility rope and at least 100 feet of Para cord. Para cord has hundreds of uses and quickly becomes indispensable. Utility rope will be useful at times you need something bigger than Para cord to accomplish your goal. Zip ties will also come in handy too.

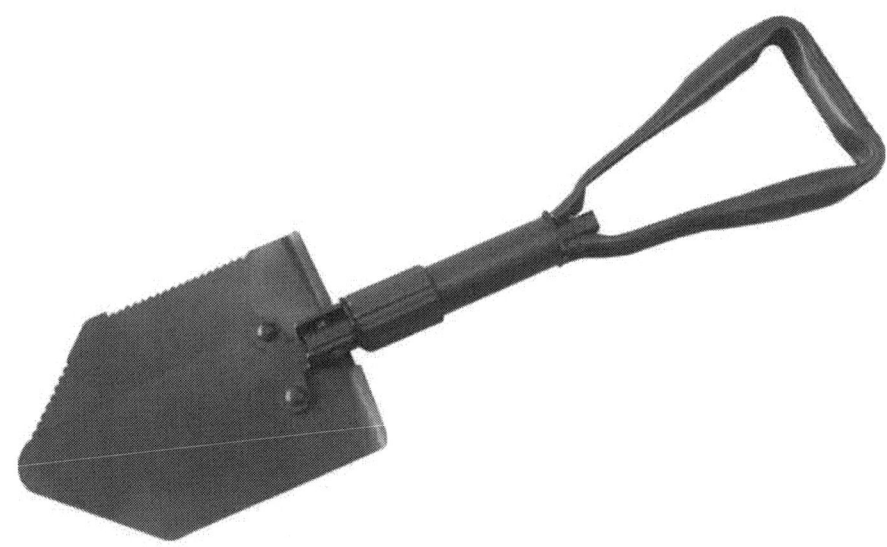

E-Tool – Also known as an entrenching tool or collapsible shovel. Besides for the obvious reasons this is another item that will have several uses. In addition to being a shovel the edge can be sharpened and can be used as an effective cutting tool.

Folding Hand Saw – Effective for cutting small trees and branches. Gathering Fire wood and cutting through frozen Ice on lakes and rivers to access fishing opportunities.

Toilet Paper – For obvious reasons and it's a lot more comfortable than using a leaf. If you have ever made the mistake of using Poison Ivy you will never make that mistake twice.

Sunscreen – For obvious reasons.

Personal Hygiene Kit – A kit with Dental floss, Tooth brush and toothpaste, hand sanitizer, Soap and Dish Soap. Feminine products for women.

Can Opener – Military P-51 preferably.

Yoyo Fish Trap – Catches fish unattended.

Collapsible Chair – keeps you up off the ground and more comfortable than sitting on a log or rock.

Carmex/Chapstic – Obvious reasons

Zip lock Bags – Useful for keeping things dry and keeping bugs out of things.

Bug Spray – Because you don't want to be something else's lunch.

Padded Ground Mat – Sleeping on the hard ground is not for everyone.

Spare Batteries – If you are not using rechargeable batteries and a solar recharger.

BioLight Camp Stove

Portable Mini Stove – Either one that works on fuel or a BioLight stove.

Books – A couple books you may want to throw in are a guide to edible plants and a basic survival guide.

Ideally you will want to carry anything you think you will need. Admittedly some of the items on this list are luxury items and can be omitted for concerns of space or weight.

CHAPTER 14

HOW TO PACK YOUR BAG

There is no particular right or wrong way to pack your 72-Hour bag. However just as with anything else it takes some planning. Think about what you will need to have access to and how often you will need to have access to it. Once you have figured that out lay out the contents of the bag and pack accordingly. I will lay out how I prefer to pack my bag for the purposes of illustrating how I pack my 72-Hour bag.

First of all on the very bottom of my pack I place my **Documentation Pack** in a large zip lock bag. On top of that is a **Tarp** then followed by my **Clothing**. Next I place my spare **Ammunition, Deck of Cards, Personal Hygiene supplies.** If your pack has compartment dividers this would be where you would use them.

In the next compartment I place my **Ice Fishing Pole** in a rod tube, **Fishing Kit, Yoyo Fish Trap, Rope and Para Cord, Mess Kit, Bartering Kit, Radio, Spice Kit, BioLight Stove,** and **Water Purification Pump**. Then I place my **Collapsible Chair, Solar Charging Panel, Food,** and both **Tactical Holsters,** and

Handguns, Jacket and **Raingear.**

In the side pockets on the pack contain **Toilet Paper, Spare Socks, Water Purification Tablets, Fire Starting Kit, Flashlight/Glow sticks, Headlamp, Whistle** and **Signal Mirror.** On the outside of the pack is attached the **CamelBak, E-Tool, First Aid Kit** and **Tactical Tomahawk.**

To the bottom of the pack are attached my **Sleeping Bag** in its stuff sack**, Tent,** and **Sleeping pad**. On the pack straps are the **GPS, Knife, Compass,** and **Binoculars** in their respective cases.

The most important thing to keep in mind when packing your pack is to think about what items you are going to use the most and those that will be used less frequently. It doesn't make sense to pack your GPS or Compass in the bottom of your pack if you have to stop and completely unpack every time you need to use it. Certain items that you may only use when setting up camp or when you are done traveling for the day will be better packed towards the bottom. In regards to the first aid kit, I find that it is best to have it quickly and easily accessible. Having it attached to the outside of the pack makes it easily accessible when needed.

It is always a good idea to test out your bag at this point once it is assembled go out and actually use it for a couple nights. Go for a hike and carry it for a prolonged period of time. This will allow you to determine if you are carrying the right amount of weight. Use all your equipment and make sure you are familiar with how they all work. This field test will be important for not only making sure you know how everything works, but will also allow you to gauge the usefulness of your equipment. You may also find it necessary to do this field test more than once. Ideally you would want to do a field test during each season to assess the usefulness of your equipment in all conditions and environments.

After a field test you will want to assess what worked well and what didn't. Make changes to any gear that didn't work well for you or the situation. If you had a particularly hard time using an item then you will want to practice using that item until you can use it effectively. This is extremely important. If you can't use a fire bow to start a fire and yet that is all you have available then you are at a disadvantage. In the middle of a crisis is not the time to try and learn how to use an item.

CHAPTER 15

PETS

Sixty percent of people own pets, and for most of them their pets are no different than their children. It is for this reason that I chose to include this chapter. When thinking about a situation where you are going to need to use your 72-Hour Bag you are probably going to be bringing your family with you. Your pets are undoubtedly going to be coming along too. You need to consider this into your planning. When thinking about your pets you will want them to carry their own supplies. The following is a general list of recommended supplies.

3 to 4 day's supply of food

1 or 2 liters of water

Collapsible water and food dish

Pet first aid kit w/Pet First Aid book

Spare Leash and Harness

Stake & Cable (if you need to tie them up)

Neoprene Dog Shoes

In an ideal scenario your dog is big enough to carry his own 72-Hour Bag. If this isn't the case, you'll simply need to incorporate the needed items into your own 72-Hour Bag. If you have a large breed, the first thing you should do is buy a good saddle back dog backpack. In most pet supply stores and sporting goods stores you can find packs for your dogs to wear and carry. Ideally you will want one that is comfortable on your dog's back. Many dog backpacks have features like removable bags or integrated water bottles to carry all of your dog's water.

Whatever pack you decide the most important thing you can do is get your dog used to wearing it. Start slowly by getting him use to wearing the empty pack, and then slowly work your way up to a full bag.

Water

There are plenty of options to carry water for your dog including water bladders, canteens or plain old plastic water bottles. Always plan to refill your dog's water supply when you are refilling your own water supply. You will also need a collapsible water dish and food dish. They are reliable, have a pull string to keep food in if necessary and fold up nice and small for easy storage.

Food

The next thing you'll need to include is food for your pet. While the type of food you should bring is a personal choice, the best option is to stick to something that will keep the weight down. There is a company that makes a product called buddy meals. Inside each package you will find: an 8 oz. bag of kibble (which is enough for 1-3 feedings, depending on the size of your dog), a 12 oz. bottle of purified water, a 2 oz. doggy treat, a waste removal bag, and a divided biodegradable serving dish.

Buddy Meals

Leash and Harness

You will also want a leash, an 8 or 12 foot should be sufficient to keep your dog close and under-control. The second piece is a bit of long cordage or cable and a ground spike in order to tie your dog up at night but leave him enough room to patrol the camp. In a pinch Para cord will work, but a determined dog can chew through it in one night.

Dog Shoes

If you are planning on moving on foot for any long distances it's good to have a spare pair of neoprene dog shoes as well. These are rugged boots made to last on tough terrain where rocks or other objects might cut into your dog's pads. They are also helpful in winter climates at preventing temperature injuries to your dog's feet. You will want to get your dog used to wearing these well in advance of any emergency situation.

Dog Boots

Pet First Aid Kit

Just like a human first aid kit is a necessity so is one for your pet. These can be bought preassembled or you can talk to your vet and get a list of items and build one yourself. Ideally you will want to include antibiotic ointment, splinter removers, examination gloves, Benadryl for allergies, and a Pet First Aid Guide. Also you will want to include a brush or comb and a good pair of pet nail clippers. This can make all the difference in the comfort level of your pooch.

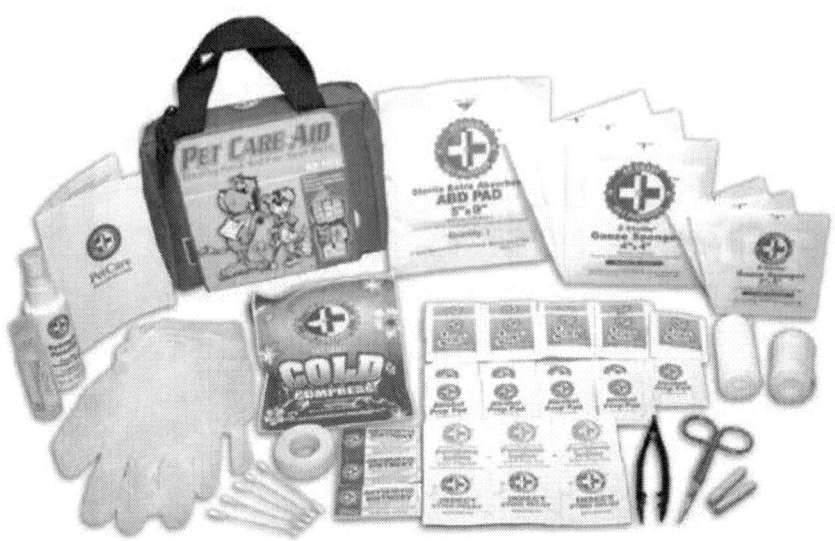

Pet First Aid Kit

Clothing

Just like people your pet will need appropriate clothing I suggest a jacket or vest and a good pair of boots. Not only will this help keep your pet warm. Since your pet will most likely be walking you will want it sturdy enough to protect them from burrs, sticks, rocks, and anything else that might cause irritation to their fur, skin, or paws.

It is easy to forget about our pets when planning your 72-Hour Bag. If you take the time to create one at the same time you are creating your own, you will be happy when you need to use it and your pet will thank you too.

CHAPTER 16

CHECKLISTS

Here is a handy checklist you can use to assemble your 72-Hour Bag. Keep in mind you can add or omit things as needed.

Clothing & Apparel
☐ Back Pack
☐ Bandana
☐ Belt (heavy duty)
☐ Dust Masks
☐ Hat
☐ Hiking Boots
☐ Long Johns (Thermal Underwear)
☐ Rain Ponchos
☐ Sleeping Bag
☐ Spare Shoe Laces
☐ Sun Glasses
☐ Sweater
☐ Underwear
☐ Winter Gloves / Mits
☐ Wool Socks (x2 pair)
☐ Wool Blanket
☐ Work Gloves

First Aid / Medical

- After Bite
- Antiseptic wipes (Alcohol and iodine)
- Antibiotics
- Bandages
- Bandage Wraps (for sprained wrists, leg, etc...)
- Benadryl (for bee and wasp stings)
- Burn Cream
- Butterfly Sutures / Bandages
- Cortisone cream (for poison ivy, etc.)
- Cotton Balls
- Decongestants (Colds)
- First Aid Manual
- Gauze Pads
- Imodium (Anti-diarrhea)
- Iodine Tablets (radiation)
- Latex / Surgical Gloves
- Lip Balm (medicated)
- Medical Tape (white)
- Nail Clippers
- Needles (for suturing, sterilize with alcohol wipes)
- Polysporin
- Quick-Clot (stops bleeding)
- Saline Nasal Spray
- Safety Pins – Various sizes
- Sewing Kit
- Sunscreen
- Surgical Blades
- Vaseline
- Tampons / Maxi Pads
- Tweezers
- Tylenol / Advil

Fire & Heat

- [ ] Candles (emergency – long burning)
- [ ] Cotton Balls (soaked in Vaseline)
- [ ] Heating Pads
- [ ] Lighters
- [ ] Flint / Magnesium Starter
- [ ] Matches
- [ ] Steel Wool (and 9v battery)
- [ ] Thermal Blankets

Food / Cooking / Water

- [ ] Aluminum Foil (about 5 feet folded)
- [ ] Aluminum bottle (carry water, boiling)
- [ ] Beef Jerky
- [ ] Can Opener
- [ ] Coffee & Filters
- [ ] Collapsible Water Container
- [ ] Energy Bars (3000 calories)
- [ ] Granola Bars
- [ ] Hose (siphoning or drinking)
- [ ] Instant Oatmeal
- [ ] Oxo Cubes
- [ ] MRE's
- [ ] Packs of condiments (ketchup, mustard, hot sauce)
- [ ] Portable Mini Stove
- [ ] Salt & Pepper
- [ ] Seeds (for planting)
- [ ] Soups
- [ ] Tea Bags
- [ ] Water Purification Tablets

Hunting & Protection

- [ ] .22 Rifles and ammo (and cleaning kit, oil)
- [ ] Binoculars
- [ ] Ammo Belt Pouch
- [ ] Arrows (wood and aluminum)
- [ ] Chain Link for fish
- [ ] Fishing Kit (Line, Lures, Jigs, Weights, Reel, Floats, Etc.)
- [ ] Fishing Rod (ice fishing length)
- [ ] Hunting Knife (and sharpening stone)
- [ ] Mosquito Head / Body Net
- [ ] Mosquito Repellant with deet
- [ ] Pepper Spray
- [ ] Sling Shot and ammo
- [ ] Snare Wire

Hygiene

- [ ] Bar of soap
- [ ] Comb
- [ ] Dental Floss
- [ ] Deodorant (non scented)
- [ ] Gold bond powder
- [ ] Razors
- [ ] Shampoo
- [ ] Maxi Pads / Tampons
- [ ] Tooth Brush (Portable)
- [ ] Toothpaste
- [ ] Toothpicks
- [ ] Toilet Paper
- [ ] Wash Cloth
- [ ] Wipes

Navigation, Signaling and Lighting

- [ ] Batteries (AA, AAA)
- [ ] Hand Crank Radio
- [ ] Head Lamp
- [ ] Flash Lights (LED)
- [ ] Fluorescent Trail Marker Tape
- [ ] Light / Glow Sticks
- [ ] Map and Compass (local area / province)
- [ ] Mirror
- [ ] Survival Manual
- [ ] Whistle

Tools & Other Equipment

- [ ] Axe (chopping axe)
- [ ] Garbage Bags (black and white)
- [ ] Duct Tape
- [ ] File (Sharpening tools, shaping wood, etc.)
- [ ] Folding saw
- [ ] Folding Shovel / Pick
- [ ] FRS Radio
- [ ] Measuring Tape & Sewing Tape
- [ ] Multi-Purpose Tool
- [ ] Padded Ground Mat
- [ ] Para cord / Rope
- [ ] Saw (Bow Saw – Collapsible)
- [ ] Small screwdriver with all bits
- [ ] Tarps (waterproof with grommet holes)
- [ ] Wire Saw
- [ ] Zip Lock Bags
- [ ] Zip Ties

Extras

- [ ] Money (Bills and a few rolls of quarters)
- [ ] Book on edible plants
- [ ] Book on Survival

ABOUT THE AUTHOR

Stephen B. Fraser (1971-) was born in Sacramento, California. While growing up in North Idaho and Western Montana he learned to appreciate the outdoors and the naturalist lifestyle. He is a confirmed realist, and student of human nature. He has written several short stories under a pen name. His first book was released in Feb 2012 under his own name. He completed his second book in October and revised and re-released his first book in November. Stephen currently resides in beautiful North Idaho with his dog Ollie where he enjoys camping, fishing, and continues to work in the Healthcare field. When he is not writing he is pursuing his other interests.

You can follow Stephen of Twitter @stephenbfraser and at stephenbfraser.com.

Other Books by Stephen B. Fraser

Men: The Handbook

Politics 101

So You Want To Be A Nursing Assistant

4572577R00056

Printed in Great Britain
by Amazon.co.uk, Ltd.,
Marston Gate.